M000195939

Catffirmations

*A Journal with Mindful Mantras
to Awaken Your Inner Cat*

Catffirmations

A Journal with Mindful Mantras to Awaken Your Inner Cat

ART BY Lim Heng Swee

CHRONICLE BOOKS

SAN FRANCISCO

Text copyright © 2023 by Chronicle Books.
Illustrations copyright © 2023 by Lim Heng Swee.

All rights reserved. No part of this product may be reproduced in any form without written permission from the publisher.

ISBN 978-1-7972-1859-5

MIX
Paper | Supporting
responsible forestry
FSC™ C136333

Manufactured in China.

Design by Evelyn Furuta.
Text by Marcello Picone.

10 9 8 7 6 5 4 3 2 1

See the full range of Catffirmations gift products at www.chroniclebooks.com.

Chronicle Books publishes distinctive books and gifts. From award-winning children's titles, bestselling cookbooks, and eclectic pop culture to acclaimed works of art and design, stationery, and journals, we craft publishing that's instantly recognizable for its spirit and creativity. Enjoy our publishing and become part of our community at www.chroniclebooks.com.

Special quantity discounts are available to corporations and other organizations. Contact our premiums department at corporatesales@chroniclebooks.com or at 1-800-759-0190.

CHRONICLE BOOKS
680 SECOND STREET
SAN FRANCISCO, CA 94107
WWW.CHRONICLEBOOKS.COM

I can

thrive

no matter

where

I am.

Picture your warm, sunny, perfectly happy place.
What does it look like?

_____

_____

_____

_____

_____

_____

_____

_____

_____

_____

_____

_____

_____

_____

_____

_____

_____

_____

_____

_____

_____

I am liquid.
I am stillness.
I'm a
**gorgeous
contradiction.**

Take a moment to imagine you have nine lives. Now describe them.

1 _____

2 _____

3 _____

4 _____

5 _____

6 _____

7 _____

8 _____

9 _____

I'm forever hanging in there.

Describe your ultimate catnip.

I am just right just where I am.

What calls forth your most ardent curiosity?

Life's obstacles are an **adventure**.

I leap in with sure-footed **confidence**.

Write about whatever brings out your fierce, ferocious side.

_____

_____

_____

_____

_____

_____

_____

_____

_____

_____

_____

_____

_____

_____

_____

_____

_____

_____

_____

_____

I've had
many lives.
And I
embrace
them all.

Who (or what) inspires in you a boundless
sense of play?

_____

_____

_____

_____

_____

_____

_____

_____

_____

_____

_____

_____

_____

_____

_____

_____

_____

_____

To live is to play.

Make a list of all the things that might drive you into hiding.

1   *Vacuum cleaner*

2

3

4

5

6

7

8

9

I will make it to the top

on my own terms.

Describe yourself in super stealth mode.

I am **grounded**.

Well, look what the cat dragged in! Describe all the guilty pleasures you're likely to bring home.

_____

_____

_____

_____

_____

_____

_____

_____

_____

_____

_____

_____

_____

_____

_____

_____

_____

_____

_____

Stress
is not in
my vocabulary.

What makes you purrrr like a kitten?

I don't have
to chase
anything
to be happy.

Describe a time you went out on a limb and came out on top.

_____

_____

_____

_____

_____

_____

_____

_____

_____

_____

_____

_____

_____

_____

_____

_____

_____

_____

_____

_____

I always seek a new
perspective.

What makes your hackles rise and your hair stand on end? Scribble down a list—then scratch them all out.

1

2

3

4

5

6   *That dog next door*

7

8

9

Inner peace

is just a

catnap away.

I feel **seen**.

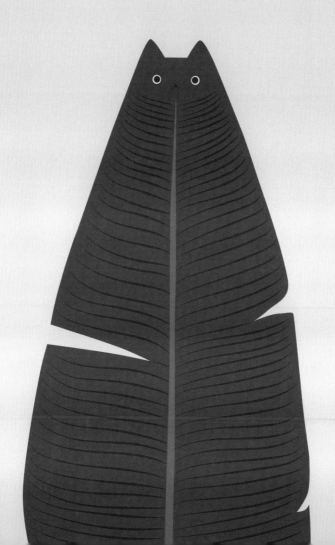

What's getting in the way of pouncing on your goals?

Sometimes
it's good to
let go.

What qualities have you kept hidden from the world?

I contain

multitudes.

Take a moment to list your favorite playthings. What (or whom) do you love to toy with?

1

2

3

4   *Ball of yarn*

5

6

7

8

9

I am calm
and confident
and
**covered in
sharp spines**

just in case.

Paint a picture of your nightlife: Are you out on the prowl, or curled up at home?

I **embrace** love
in my own way.

What's new, pussycat?

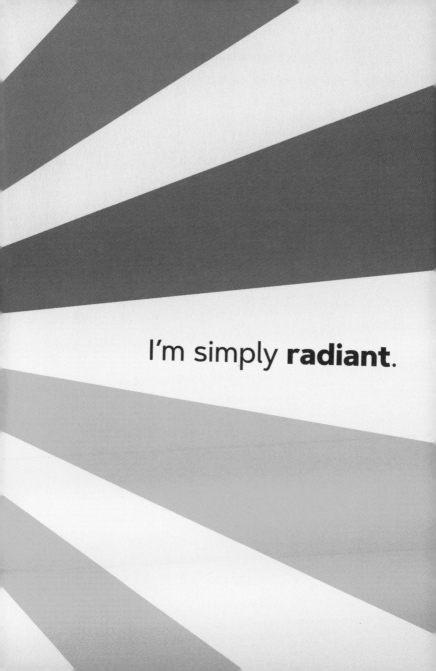

I'm simply **radiant**.

Imagine taking a breathtaking leap of faith.
What would it feel like and where will you land?

Every change is an **opportunity**.

I **know** I will land on my feet.

You are a natural hunter. Describe a time you captured the ultimate, elusive prey.

If you don't
get me,
I have to go
be **awesome**
elsewhere.

What is it about yourself that you're most proud of?
And what are you just a little too proud of?

_____

_____

_____

_____

_____

_____

_____

_____

_____

_____

_____

_____

_____

_____

_____

_____

_____

_____

_____

_____

All roads lead to relaxing.

Make a list of all the things that can distract you.

1 _____

2 *Red laser pointer* _____

3 _____

4 _____

5 _____

6 _____

7 _____

8 _____

9 _____

_____

_____

Lean into

the eternal

flow of

time.

Describe an itch you're absolutely dying to scratch.

I ride the wave.
A wave that rises
with great power.

I am the wave.
A wave that crests,
knowing its direction.

Paint a picture of yourself as the fearless, gravity-defying creature you know yourself to be.

I reach out
with curiosity.

Is there anyone or anything you'd be perfectly fine to ignore for the rest of your life?

_____

_____

_____

_____

_____

_____

_____

_____

_____

_____

_____

_____

_____

_____

_____

_____

_____

_____

_____

You're clever, playful, and insatiably curious. How do you stay so cool, kitty cat?

I.

Am.

Magnificent.